To Oprah With Love

To Oprah With Love

A TRIBUTE

Photographs

by

PAUL

NATKIN

and

STEPHEN

GREEN

NEW MILLENNIUM
PRESS

ISBN: 1-893224-63-5
Printed in the United Kingdom

New Millennium Press
301 N. Canon Drive, Suite 214
Beverly Hills, CA 90210

Library of Congress Cataloging-in-Publication Data
available from the publisher

Book Design 2002 by Michele Lanci-Altomare

10 9 8 7 6 5 4 3 2 1

I first met Oprah Winfrey when she was hosting her television show in Baltimore in 1980. I was a guest on the show, and she surprised me by having my daughter picked up from the school she was attending so she could make a surprise appearance from behind a curtain during my segment. This lovely gesture certainly brought some pleasure to her dad. Oprah has been surprising and pleasing millions in the years since that day more than twenty years ago.

Since she moved on to conquer Chicago and her program expanded nationally she's become an incredible force in the world of media. Oprah could have been anything she wanted: business executive, actress, host, book or magazine editor. Instead, she decided to do it all. You look up "daytime talk" in the dictionary and you get a picture of Oprah Winfrey.

She's also one hell of a broad: gutsy, determined, kind, and someone who relates incredibly well to her audience. They know and love her as a friend.

Here's a dandy collection of Oprah's many incarnations. In some photos she's slim, in others not so slim, but she always has that infectious smile that lights up any room. In the rare world of one-word names, all you need to know is Oprah. Whatever happened to Winfrey, anyway?

LARRY KING

Oprah and many of the wonderful guests we photographed

Caroline Kennedy Schlossberg

John F. Kennedy, Jr.

Senator Hillary Rodham Clinton

President Jimmy Carter and First Lady Rosalynn Carter

Former mayor Harold Washington

Mayor Richard M. Daley

Former governor Ann Richards

Reverend Al Sharpton

Ice-T and Tipper Gore

Steve Martin

Dan Aykroyd and Steve Martin

Diane Keaton, Bette Midler, and Goldie Hawn

Bette Midler

Goldie Hawn

Danny Glover

Danny Glover and Spike Lee

Steven Spielberg

Jaid Barrymore and Drew Barrymore

Tom Cruise

Robin Williams

Sissy Spacek, Demi Moore, and Cher

Cher

Michael Douglas and Danny DeVito

Meryl Streep

Robert DeNiro and Meryl Streep

James Earl Jones

Tom Hanks

Don Johnson and Kevin Costner

Kevin Costner

Tim Robbins and Susan Sarandon

Elizabeth Taylor

Sylvester Stallone and Kurt Russell

Sylvester Stallone

Eddie Murphy

Bruce Willis

Arnold Schwarzenegger

Kathleen Turner

Whoopi Goldberg

Warren Beatty and Annette Bening

Shirley MacLaine

Cast of *Steel Magnolias;* Shirley MacLaine, Sally Field, Dolly Parton, Daryl Hannah, Olympia Dukakis, Julia Roberts

Ethan Hawke

Maya Angelou

Maya Angelou and Alice Walker

Jacqueline Mitchard and the first Oprah Bookclub

Gloria Steinem

Murphy Brown cast; Charles Kimbrough, Grant Shaud, Candace Bergen, Joe Regalbuto, Faith Ford, Robert Pastorelli, Pat Corley

Candace Bergen

Dudley Moore and Liza Minelli

Liza Minelli

Tony Bennett and Liza Minelli

Tony Bennett, Liza Minelli, and Michael Bolton

Michael Bolton

Whitney Houston

Cast of *Waiting to Exhale* and the author; Lela Rochon, Loretta Devine, Angela Bassett, Whitney Houston, Terry McMillan

Oleta Adams

Kenneth "Babyface" Edmonds

Brandi

Quincy Jones
Mark Wahlberg
TLC
Mark Wahlberg and TLC
En Vogue
New Edition
Stevie Wonder
Aaron Neville, Mariah Carey, and Amy Grant
Mariah Carey
Aaron Neville
Liberace
Elvis impersonators
Barry Manilow
Ashley, Wynonna, and Naomi Judd
Clint Black
Wynonna, K.T. Oslin, Clint Black, Kathy Mattea, and Naomi Judd
Dolly Parton
Kenny Rogers
Julio Iglesias
Paul Stanley, Gene Simmons, Jackie Collins, and Pamela DesBarres
Natalie Cole
Luther Vandross
Evander Holyfield
Michael Jordan
Michael Jordan and Scottie Pippin
Terry Bradshaw, George Brett, Hank Aaron, and Walter Payton
Earvin "Magic" Johnson, Cookie Johnson and their son Earvin, Jr.
Al Joyner and Florence Griffith Joyner
Reggie Miller
The Harlem Globetrotters
Martha Stewart
Ted Koppel
Barbara Walters
Jane Wagner, Lily Tomlin and Barbara Walters

Jane Pauley
Meredith Viera
John Tesh and Mary Hart
Billy Crystal
Rosie O'Donnell
Shirley Hemphill and Rosie O'Donnell
Jay Leno
Bob Hope
Michael J. Fox
Al Franken as Stewart Smalley
Bill Cosby
Bill Cosby, Keshia Knight Pulliam and Raven Symone
Paul Reiser
Cast of *Twister*; Jami Gertz, Bill Paxton and Helen Hunt
Tim Allen
Kevin Meany, Jerry Seinfeld, Dave Coulier and Lenny Clarke
Roseanne
Roseanne and Tom Arnold
Cast of *Friends;* Lisa Kudrow, Matthew Perry, Courtney Cox
Arquette, David Schwimmer, Jennifer Aniston and Matt LeBlanc
Roger Ebert
Fran Drescher
Kenny Ortega
Susan Lucci and her husband Helmut Huber, Stedman Graham,
Barbara Mandrell and her husband Ken Dudney
Oprah, Stedman Graham and their beloved Cocker Spaniel Sophie
Burt Reynolds
Linda Evans and Yanni
Linda Evans
Rosie Daley
Bob Greene
Esther Williams
Donna Karan
Cindy Crawford
Baby Jessica (Jessica McClure) and her parents

A man may die, nations may rise and fall, but an idea lives on.

JOHN F. KENNEDY

I dwell in Possibility.

EMILY DICKINSON

A wise man will make more opportunities than he finds.

SIR FRANCIS BACON

ILFORD HP5

2   2A   3   3A

2   7   ILFORD HP5   ILFORD HP5

5   5A   6   6A   7   7A

38

Imagination will often carry us to worlds that never were.

But without it, we go nowhere.

L. FRANK BAUM

*G*ive me somewhere to stand, and I will move the earth.

ARCHIMEDES

The best and most beautiful things in the world cannot be seen or even touched—they must be felt with the heart.

HELEN KELLER

*A*ll my life I have fought against prejudice and intolerance.

HARRY S. TRUMAN

85

...joy delights in joy...

WILLIAM SHAKESPEARE

$\mathcal{W}$e love the things we love

for what they are.

ROBERT FROST

Through music the passions enjoy themselves.

FREDERICK NEITZSCHE

*M*usic washes away from the soul the dust of everyday life.

WILLIAM CONGREVE

YAMAHA

*B*elieve that life is worth living, and your belief will help create the fact.

WILLIAM JAMES

129

There is a spirituality about the face, however…which the typewriter does not generate. The lady is a musician.

$\mathcal{A}$ *good laugh is sunshine in a house.*

WILLIAM MAKEPEACE THACKERAY

It's kind of fun to do the impossible.

*A*lways do right. This will gratify some people, and astonish the rest.

—— MARK TWAIN

$\mathcal{I}$t is not enough to have a good mind.

The main thing is to use it well.

RENE DESCARTES

We must be the change we wish to see in the world.

There is no instinct like that of the heart.

— LORD BYRON

201

There is no wisdom like frankness.

BENJAMIN DISRAELI

*M*ake *yourself necessary to someone.*

RALPH WALDO EMERSON

$\mathcal{B}$*eauty is Nature's brag, and must be shown…*

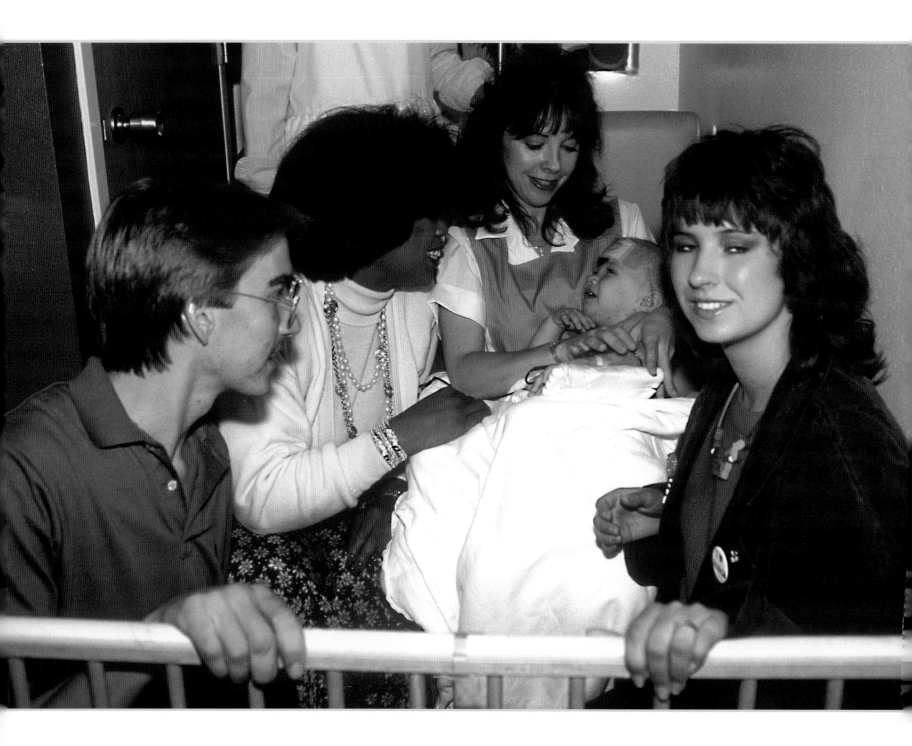

$\mathcal{W}$hat a fantastic journey we have had!

From 1986 to 1996, we shared the extraordinary progress of a cultural icon. We saw, and had the opportunity to capture, the deep levels of trust that Oprah enjoys with her audience, her viewers and her many guests. During those years as staff photographers, we witnessed her influence grow and watched how her interests and personal evolution paralleled and spurred those of her devoted viewers.

We traveled with her to the homes of movie stars and celebrated with her over everything from weight loss to personal and spiritual growth. We were amazed by the way she confronted street gangs and provocative issues alike, with purpose. As with her other fans, we were intrigued by her skill and comfort with everyone, from presidential candidates to literary luminaries. We aimed our lenses at her strengths and her vulnerabilities, and came to know a lot about what made Oprah "America's Girlfriend".

Our unique access and intimacy provided us with this very personal photographic diary and a great dilemma. What pictures should we cull out of a vast selection of portraits for this book? Which favorite memories will we revive or leave unrevealed? We hope that our choices have offered you a glimpse of your own treasured experiences.

PAUL NATKIN AND STEPHEN GREEN